S   RS

The Snoops

For my son, Finn– M.M.
Pour "La Gloute" – D.D.

A TEMPLAR BOOK

First published in the UK in hardback in 1997 by Templar Publishing
This edition published in 2003 by Templar Publishing,
an imprint of The Templar Company plc,
Pippbrook Mill, London Road, Dorking, Surrey, RH4 1JE, UK
www.templarco.co.uk

Distributed in the UK by Ragged Bears Ltd.,
Ragged Appleshaw, Andover, Hampshire, SP11 9HX

First softback edition

ISBN 1-84011-146-1

Designed by Mike Jolley

Printed in Hong Kong

The Snoops

by **Miriam Moss**

illustrated by **Delphine Durand**

templar publishing

The Snoops live
at number nine Keyhole Crescent.
They are the street busybodies
who pry and peek and nose out
everybody's secrets.

At a whiff of a whisper
they prick up their ears,
hang on words,
drink in rumours.

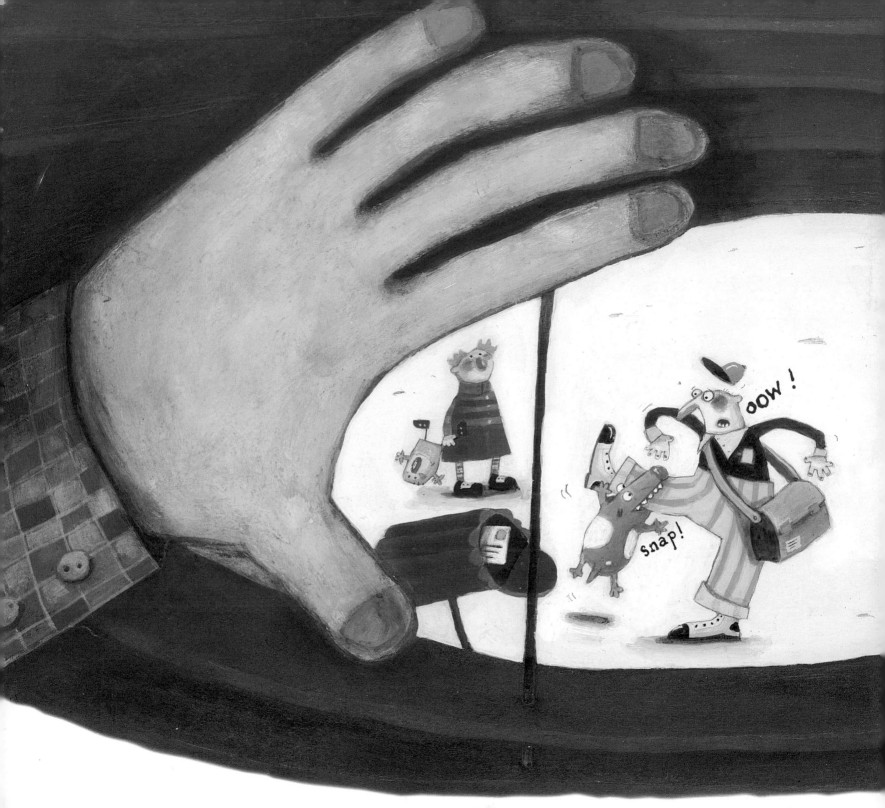

At the hint of a **raised** voice they are on their toes.

itching with interest, burning with curiosity.

Or the price tag
     on Tilly Toddler's new shoes,
          Or old Miss Spankie (who's lost her hanky)
               wiping her nose on her sleeve.

They spy Mr. Cramp tipping buckets of snails over the fence...

...into Batty Matty's moonlit garden.

And then watch Batty Matty painting
Mr. Cramp's Cat.

They see the silent unscrewing of Mrs. McCafferty's gate

and watch it appear, newly painted, in Handy Andy's back garden.

as Miss McBride reverses into Mr. Hornby's new car.

clatter

splinter

They hear drumming footsteps,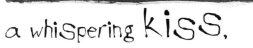

a whispering **KISS,**   the flick of a light,

the slam of a dOor,

THWUMP

and spot
Slippery Sam
Sliding off through
the bushes.

They hear
Colonel Blink's tyres hissing flat
as Tricky Dicky flicks
his pocketknife closed
and saunters off.

They hear
the snagging tear
of Mr. James' trousers
ripping on a drainpipe
after he's been locked out.

RRRIP!

The Snoops have sharp noses.

When Dotty Miles' pig disappears
they trace the smell of bacon cooking
back to Fatty Hardy's kitchen.

They even sniff out which dog
did which poo where,
and plot it on a graph.

But...
The Snoops have one gigantic fear.
They are terrified of being snooped on themselves!

To keep their spirits up,
they sing a snooping song
in low, trumpety voices.

Now everyone in Keyhole Crescent
was fed up with being Snooped on.
And, despite all their snooping,
the Snoops never guessed.

So they didn't find out about
the Secret meeting
in the café
round the corner.

They just watched everyone return in dribs and drabs, nudging each other

and nodding up at number **nine**. This made the Snoops nervous and unse**t**tled.

So they snooped even harder.

And they were so busy snooping that they didn't even notice..